Wayne Gretzky
The Great Goodbye

Wayne Gretzky

The Great Goodbye

Edited by Scott Morrison

KEY PORTER BOOKS

Key Porter Books gratefully acknowledges the following sources for permission to reproduce photographs:
Sun Media Corporation: pages 9, 12, 13, 17, 23–29, 31, 32, 33, 36–41, 50, 51, 55-57, 60-63, 65-71, 76–79.
Canadian Press: pages 10, 11, 19, 21, 22, 30, 34, 42–45, 47–49, 52, 53, 58, 59, 72, 73, 80–85.

A special thank-you to all the writers, editors and photographers in the Sun Media chain who did such a marvelous job of covering The Great One from start to finish.

Canadian Cataloguing in Publication Data

Morrison, Scott
        Gretzky : the great goodbye

ISBN 1-55263-099-4

1. Gretzky, Wayne, 1961-   2. Hockey players – Canada – Biography.
I. Title.

GV848.5.G78M67 1999   796.962'092   C99-931197-2

The publisher gratefully acknowledges the support of the Canada Council for the Arts and the Ontario Arts Council for its publishing program.

We acknowledge the financial support of the Government of Canada through the Book Publishing Industry Development Program (BPIDP) for our publishing activities.

Canada

Key Porter Books Limited
70 The Esplanade
Toronto, Ontario
Canada M5E 1R2

www.keyporter.com

Distributed in the United States by Firefly books

Design: Peter Maher
Editor: Glen Williams
Copy editor: John Sweet
Formatting: Patricia Cavazzini
Editorial assistant: Alison Young
Production assistant: Karen Bond

Printed and bound in Canada

99 00 01 02 03   6 5 4 3 2

Contents

Introduction   6

Farewell   8

The Early Years   18

Edmonton: The Glory Days   24

Hockey in the Sun Belt   36

St. Louis   46

99 in the Big Apple   54

Captain Canada   64

The Last Goodbye   74

Introduction

Perhaps the saddest thing about Wayne Gretzky's final game in the National Hockey League was that, well, they had to go ahead and actually play the damn thing. It was sad, first and foremost, because it meant that the illustrious career of the most prolific scorer in NHL history, the greatest player ever in at least one man's opinion, had drawn to an end on the afternoon of Sunday, April 18 — and finality always is sad.

Even though Gretzky wanted his departure to be more of a celebration than a funeral, there often is a profound sense of sorrow before there is joy, and so it was on April 18. As NHL commissioner Gary Bettman put it that day, "We're not ready to celebrate. It's time to be sad." Happily, there was no sense that Gretzky had made the wrong career decision. He spoke volumes when, looking weary from an emotional farewell week, he reminded everyone that he isn't the same player he was 20 years ago, or even 10 years ago, or maybe even just a couple of years ago. And we all got the point.

"It was time," he repeated. All the same, there was sadness with his announcement. It's not that we ever really took Gretzky for granted, but too often we don't fully appreciate something incredibly special until it is too late. Although someone new may eventually come along to capture our imaginations, even to make us draw comparisons with Gretzky, it will never be the same, and it will be hard for anyone to have the same skill, class, character, dignity and sense of who he is and where he came from. So it was OK to feel sad on April 18, especially when you saw the tears in Gretzky's eyes, especially when you saw the famous pair of nines on his back disappear into the dressing room for the final time.

What a ride the kid from Brantford has taken all of us on over the years. Along the way in his career — from Edmonton to Hollywood to St. Louis to Broadway — he helped win four Stanley Cup championships and three Canada Cup tournaments. He won 10 NHL scoring titles and nine Hart Trophies as the league's most valuable player. Most significantly, Gretzky holds virtually every NHL offensive record imaginable. He had that few feet of ice between the end boards and the net designated his "office." In total, he owns 61 league records. Beyond that, after being traded from Edmonton to

Los Angeles on August 9, 1988, his presence in the United States is widely accepted as the catalyst for the NHL's expansion across the sun belt.

We all know of the humble beginnings, of course: his growing up in Brantford, first starting to skate at age three on his backyard rink, playing on a team of 10-year-olds when he was only five, scoring 378 goals and 120 assists in 69 games in 1971–72, when he was just 10. And then there were the scoring exploits in the NHL, surpassing his boyhood idol Gordie Howe as the career points leader. To put all the numbers into some sort of perspective, he finished his career with more *assists* (1,963) than the next leading scorer, Howe, had *points* (1,850). It is safe to say that the NHL record book will not be requiring a rewrite of the Gretzky pages any time soon, if ever.

Beyond everything he accomplished on the ice, Gretzky was every bit as much The Great One off the ice. For those of us who had the chance to get to know him over the years, one of the best things you can say about Wayne Gretzky is that he is a magnificent person and a great Canadian. And that is saying a lot. Gretzky the person is so much the antithesis of the modern-day superstar athlete because of his thoughtfulness, his humble nature, his compassion, his remarkable attention to detail, the way he makes sure the right thing and the right person are always taken care of.

Put all of that together, all of that greatness, all of those incredible moments, and what made that damn final game so sad was how it played out, because it didn't do justice to many of the 1,486 games that preceded it. When it ended, The Great One, with an assist in his pocket, was sitting on the bench as the winning goal was being scored — by the wrong team. And just like that, it was over. After the cheers and the tears, after two curtain calls, the kid who was too small, too slight and too slow ever to make it departed after his 21st professional season. No matter: we all know that Gretzky will always be The Great One. He became a part of the fabric of the game, a player who transcended his sport, the greatest player ever and the game's greatest ambassador. You can bet that we will miss him, too. Maybe in his final season, his final game, he was more old Gretzky than the Gretzky of old, but whenever you saw No. 99 on the ice there was always the expectation of something special about to happen, and usually those expectations were met. So, yes, we'll miss him. But he will always be a part of the game in some way and we'll never forget him, because he has left us with so many memories — snapshots in our mind, snapshots on the pages that follow. Maybe now it is time to celebrate.

Farewell

An assist in final game

By AL STRACHAN — *Toronto Sun*

NEW YORK — More than an hour after his final game had ended Wayne Gretzky, still wearing his Rangers jersey, held his final media conference as a National Hockey League player.

This one was not as emotional as the one on Friday nor as dramatic as the one on Thursday. But it still was vintage Gretzky — frank, insightful and articulate. He spoke about the game itself, which ended up a 2–1 overtime victory for the Pittsburgh Penguins, and he repeatedly mentioned that he felt bad for the opponents. They were still trying to gain an advantage in the NHL playoffs, he said, and there was a danger of them being caught up in the festivities. He knew that they wanted to win but at the same time, out of respect, they didn't want to hit him. He felt that he owed it to his fans to play his best. Finally, Jaromir Jagr settled the matter with an overtime goal, which Gretzky saw as just. "Maybe it was only fitting that the best young player in the game got the goal," Gretzky said. The torch was passed "and he caught it."

When Jagr, who also has a sense of occasion, embraced Gretzky after the game, he said, "I didn't mean to do that." Gretzky laughed and told him, "That's what I used to say." As might have been expected Gretzky got an assist on the only Rangers goal of the afternoon, scored by captain Brian Leetch — who was greeted by chants of "Sign him, sign him," when he was introduced during the pregame ceremony. Gretzky admitted he found it difficult to play the game, but he managed to keep his emotions under control until late in the proceedings when Rangers coach John Muckler called a time out. "He's got a daughter who was about to give birth in Edmonton," Gretzky said. "I came over and he said, 'I tell you something.' I said, 'What?' He said, 'I just had a grandson today and you've got to get the winner.' Maybe when I was younger, I might have got that winner for him. I didn't get it today and I know it's the right time [to retire]."

Even so, even though he is convinced he has made the right

After his final game on Sunday, April 18, 1999, The Great One bid a final farewell to the Madison Square Garden faithful.

decision, he admitted that "It's going to kill me not to play. But time does something to you and it's time. I feel really confident about my decision. I haven't wavered once in seven days."

So now the retirement of Wayne Gretzky officially is under way. Today, he's going to go bowling with his teammates, an outing that was arranged a week ago when none of them knew of his intentions. Over the next few months, he's going to do some traveling and some golfing. He'll listen to offers from people who would like to have him associated with their business ventures, but he probably won't accept any for a year or more. He might end up owning a Canadian franchise, he said. Then again, he might not. For the foreseeable future, he intends to continue to live in New York.

When he was talking about the Mercedes that was given to him yesterday, he referred to the Jack Nicholson movie *A Few Good Men*. He laughed and said, "What was the line that Nicholson said? 'I think I earned it.'"

With a playoff position hanging in the balance, the Penguins check the superstar closely.

Going to the bench after his final shift, Gretzky takes a long look back at the Rangers' zone.

After scoring the overtime winner, Jaromir Jagr embraces Gretzky.

Taking the ice for his first shift of the game, No. 99 waves to his fans.

With teammate Mathieu Schneider: Gretzky celebrates his final point as an NHL player.

**An emotional Gretzky acknowledges his fans as they salute him with
a standing ovation.**

Sharing a final moment together, the Rangers pose for a team picture at center ice.

Longtime friend and Rangers coach John Muckler shares a moment with Gretzky at his final practice.

The Early Years

The first Wayne Gretzky story

This is the first story about Wayne Gretzky ever to appear in a major publication. It was written by former *Toronto Sun* hockey writer John Iaboni, and appeared in the *Toronto Telegram*'s minor hockey report on Thursday, October 28, 1971. Although many people acknowledged young Gretzky's talents at the time, few would have predicted the superstar strata that he has attained. Many items have been written chronicling his heroics since this report appeared. Many more, no doubt, will follow.

BY JOHN IABONI — *Toronto Telegram*

BRANTFORD — There's a Little No. 9 in this town who has ambitions of replacing the recently retired Big No. 9 of the Detroit Red Wings, Gordie Howe. And, as with his hero's prowess in finding the net and beating rival goaltenders, 10-year-old Wayne Gretzky has proven he can score goals, too. Now in his fifth novice A season with Brantford's Nadrofsky Steelers, the four-foot 10-inch, 70-pound defenseman-winger-center has noticed 369 goals thus far. That's including a five-goal and two-assist performance last Saturday at North Park Arena, which paced Nadrofsky to its seventh consecutive pre-season win, 7–4 over the league unbeaten MTHL Toronto Kings West Hill Highland Farms. The goal production currently stands at 41 for the 1971–72 campaign with league action in the Brantford-participating Hub League scheduled to commence in two weeks. Wayne impressed his coaches in his initial tryout when he was five years old. He earned a center berth in the 10-and-under novice league then and scored one goal while his team captured the group title. The following season, Gretzky upped his goals total to 27 as Brantford once again won the group championship. Prior to the 1969–70 season, Nadrofsky coach Bob Hockin presented Wayne with the No. 9 sweater and Gretzky responded with a 105-goal performance as a defenseman to lead Brantford to the group crown. Last year as a penalty killer, power play specialist, center and defenseman, Wayne collected a phenomenal 196 goals as Nadrofsky won the Ontario championship. Along with his list of

team and individual firsts, Wayne was selected as All-Star each season. Achievements of this sort certainly deserve a few hearty boasts, but the Grade 5 student at Greenbrier Public School remains a very modest young man. He really enjoys hockey and doesn't mind playing every shift if coach Hockin asks him to. Yes Bobby Orr, Phil Esposito and Bobby Hull are good hockey players, but as for the first two he doesn't like Boston and with the latter he is entranced only with his slapshot. "Now Gordie Howe is my kind of player. He had so many tricks around the net no wonder he scored so many goals," Gretzky said. "I'd like to be just like him. And if I couldn't play hockey I'd like to play baseball with the Oakland Athletics and Vida Blue." "Wayne is a wonderful little hockey player," Hockin said. "He ends up being more of a team player than most people realize. I know that some say he's played too often, but every time he's out there he's a threat because he controls the game. With Wayne being so dangerous and in possession of the puck quite often, he is in a position to shoot himself or set up his teammates. This is good for team morale — the others know he's giving 150 percent so they try to give 115 percent." Brantford's seven pre-season games have been typical of Wayne's consistent 150 percent efforts. While most victories have been relatively easy (11–2 over Waterford, 23–0 over Grimsby, 17–0 over Galt, 16–1 over Guelph and 13–2 over Hamilton) Nadrofsky's encounters with Toronto teams have provided spectators with close, exciting games. And each time, Gretzky has come through to give Brantford the final edge, with three goals in a 5–3 victory over powerful Don Valley Jack's Pack and again versus the Kings. Wayne was on the ice for 40 of the 45-minute Kings game and tested Toronto goalies Glen Wagg in the first period and Steve Bochum in the final two periods with 18 of his team's 31 shots on goal to account for his high points total. When Gretzky wasn't shooting at the goalies he was close to the goal area anticipating a possible rebound or congratulating wingers Brian Croley and Len Hachborn when each finished Wayne's rushes with goals. "To be very honest, I don't like to see him out on the ice all the time," said Wayne's father Walter, who is coach of the Niagara District League Junior B entry. "I'll leave the coaching up to Bob Hockin. Wayne has always been a good skater, although he's never had the size. As long as he likes the sport, I won't complain." In the Kings' dressing room, coach Pat Volpe expressed contentment in his team's play and praised Gretzky. "There's no doubt about it, he's a good hockey player," Volpe said. "They've got a fine team and we're hoping to get them back into Toronto if we can get some ice time." Judging by the solid body-checking, splendid goaltending and

Eleven-year-old Wayne meets his idol Gordie Howe, at a Great Men of Sports dinner held by the Kiwanis Club in Brantford, May 4, 1972.

Brantford's young star in 1972.

superb skating evidenced in the first Steelers–Kings encounter, a rematch in Toronto could fill the arena. A breakaway goal by Gretzky at 2:35 and a beautiful two-on-one passing play from Wayne to Croley at 13:30 gave Brantford a 2–1 first period lead. Art Robbins beat goalie George Hotston at 3:39 for a Kings goal. Goals by John Goodwin and Frankie Hachborn and Gretzky put the Steelers in front after the second period. Center Goodwin, by far the Kings' best player, tied the score after 32 seconds of the final period. But Gretzky won the game with goals at 9:08, 12:28 and 14:59. As the players congratulated each other before heading for the dressing room, Darren Thompson, an eight-year-old spectator, asked if your correspondent was a newspaper reporter. "Yes," came the reply. "Oh, are you going to write a book on Wayne Gretzky, he's good you know." No Darren, not yet, but maybe someday, soon.

Signing a twenty-one-year contract creates a media stir as a teenaged Gretzky becomes an Edmonton Oiler in 1979.

Edmonton: The Glory Days

Always an Oiler

By TERRY JONES — *Edmonton Sun*

NEW YORK — No matter how many teams a pro athlete plays for in his career, there is always one uniform he'll wear for eternity. Wayne Gretzky will always wear No. 99 with the Edmonton Oilers logo on the front. For a decade it has hurt to watch the greatest player in the history of hockey play in other uniforms. He put Edmonton on the map. Thousands here felt like they knew him. It felt, for so many people who were able to get so close and personal, like he was almost a member of the family. It has hurt to watch him play in those other cities and those other uniforms. And Gretzky said it always hurt to come back to Edmonton because he couldn't look in the crowd and not see a familiar face. But now, in a weird sort of way, he goes back to being an Edmonton Oiler again. For the ages. Now that he's called it a career, now that the great score keeper comes to write against his name, he must write that it was with the Oilers where he won lasting fame. It was in Edmonton where we watched The Greatest at his greatest. It's where he broke most of his 61 records. It's where he won his four Stanley Cups. Today you realize that it'll be as an Edmonton Oiler that Wayne Gretzky will live forever. Fifty years from now, it'll be a trivia question that he once played for the St. Louis Blues. It'll be a footnote that he finished with the New York Rangers. It'll be a testimonial that it was as a Los Angeles King that he sold the sport to so many corners of the United States where it hadn't been before. But when it comes to the essence of who he was and what he accomplished, most of the major memories — the moments which will live forever — were in Edmonton.

The eighties were indeed glory years as the Oilers' young captain led the team to four Stanley Cup victories.

The many faces of Gretzky, who is stopped by New York Islanders goaltender Billy Smith (below).

A family portrait with the
Stanley Cup.

One of many celebrations with
linemate Jari Kurri.

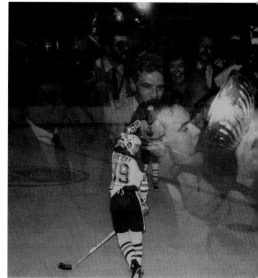

Gretzky waves to an appreciative Northlands Coliseum crowd.

He hoists the Campbell Bowl after winning a conference title.

Gretzky prepares to take a sip from the Cup.

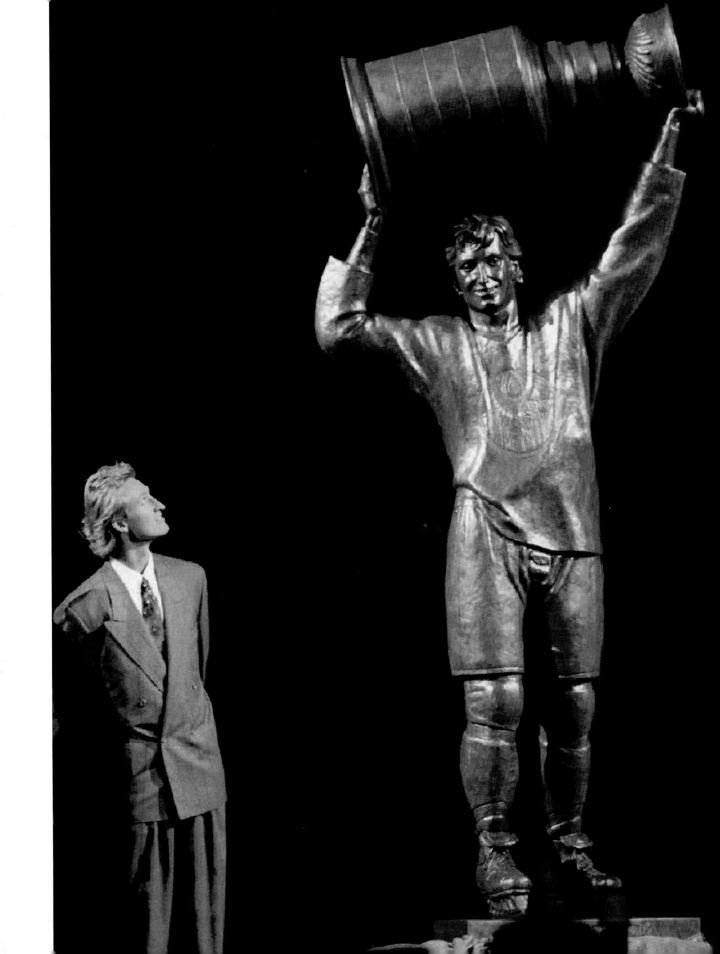

**The Oilers' captain hoists the
Stanley Cup high overhead with
a little help from his friends.**

**Gretzky surveys a statue of himself at
Northlands Coliseum following its unveiling
in Edmonton in 1989.**

Gretzky's 1988 wedding to actress
Janet Jones was a regal affair in
Edmonton.

A young and spirited team, the Oilers
enjoyed themselves on and
off the ice.

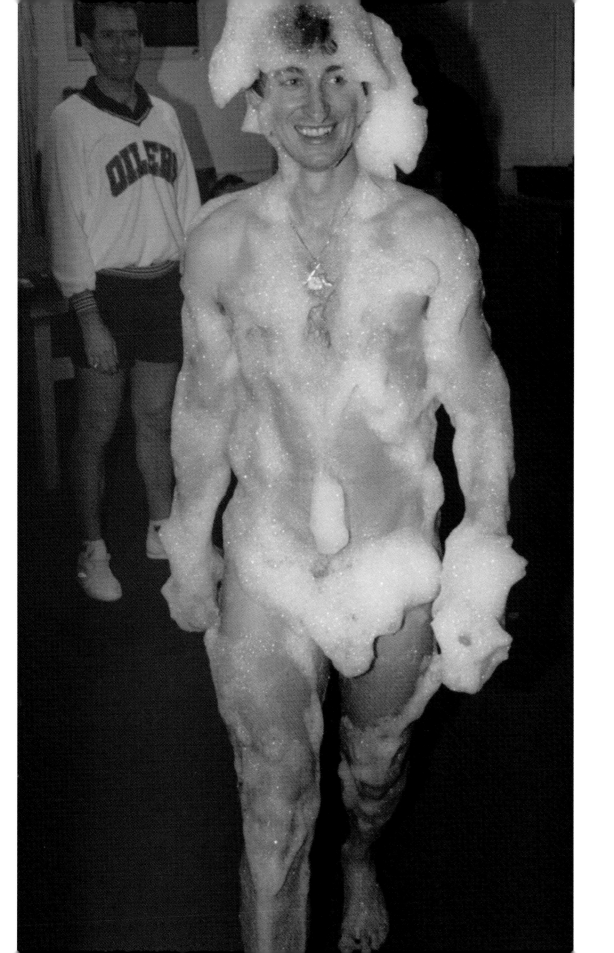

Overcome by emotion at the press conference announcing his controversial trade from Edmonton to Los Angeles on August 9, 1988.

Wayne Gretzky traded ...
... California, here he comes

BY SCOTT MORRISON — *Toronto Sun*

The King is dead. Long live the King. The tearful end to one of the most spectacular chapters in hockey history was authored in Edmonton yesterday, fittingly with one of the greatest trades involving one of the greatest players. Wayne Gretzky, the king of modern-day hockey, was dealt by the Edmonton Oilers as part of a multi-player, multi-dollar deal, one that granted his wish for a new life with the Los Angeles Kings. And, the *Sun* has learned, the trade also involves equity. Gretzky was to receive a 10% ownership share in the team but if league bylaws preclude that, he would receive a payment in the area of $5 million U.S., plus a share in gate receipts from the expected rise in the Kings' attendance from an average last season of about 10,000. The latter is part of a new, four-year contract Gretzky is expected to sign soon.

Gretzky, owner of four Stanley Cup rings, countless league scoring records, eight consecutive most valuable player awards, and other honors with the Oilers, was — at his request — sent to the Kings along with defenseman Marty McSorley and center Mike Krushelnyski. Gretzky demanded that McSorley, a noted enforcer, be included in the trade. In return for the best player in hockey, the Oilers received center Jimmy Carson, a 55-goal scorer last season, rookie left winger Martin Gélinas, the Kings' first-round draft picks in 1989, 1991 and 1993, as well as $15 million Canadian.

News of the trade set off something of an emotional earthquake. In Ottawa, NDP house leader Nelson Riis asked the government to block the trade. The impact was felt most, though, in Edmonton, and especially by Gretzky and Oilers coach/general manager Glen Sather, both of whom wept openly during a press conference.

"For the benefit of Wayne Gretzky, my new wife and our expected child in the new year," began Wayne Gretzky, who will soon begin to renegotiate a new contract with the Kings, "I thought it was beneficial to all involved if they let me play with the Kings. It's disappointing having to leave Edmonton" — pause to wipe away the tears — "but there comes a time when ..." When a new bride who lives in Hollywood, money and family become the compelling interests in a 27-year-old's life.

A man who is always giving, yesterday Gretzky took a little something for himself. Responding to the obvious insinuation that his bride of three weeks, actress Janet Jones, had insisted upon the move, Gretzky strongly denied it. "It's my own gut feeling," he said.

Although an incredibly difficult trade to finally agree to completing, Oilers owner Peter Pocklington ultimately settled two pressing needs: his own urgency for money and Gretzky's wish to move on. Over the past few seasons, Pocklington has said he would trade his superstar for cash, but waited for Gretzky's blessing. The past three years, the Kings have made overtures three separate times, New York Rangers expressed a rich interest once, and last year talks were held with the Vancouver Canucks regarding a Gretzky trade involving large amounts of cash.

"It's like losing a son, more than a hockey player," said Pocklington. "I have mixed emotions and a heavy heart." But Pocklington has also restored order to his payroll, which became severely bloated last summer when he signed Gretzky to a five-year personal services contract, paying him $1.4 million next season, and allowing him to retire in two years. The ripple effect soon followed, with Paul Coffey, Mark Messier and Grant Fuhr all asking for big money. It's strongly believed the deal was consummated between Pocklington, with Sather having only a small say, and new Kings sole owner Bruce McNall, who was bent on acquiring a big name. He got the biggest.

Now 27, Gretzky will end his career in L.A. in four years. He is also coming off a season in which he missed 16 games through injury, finished second in the scoring race for the first time in eight years (149 points) and failed to win the Hart Trophy for the first time in nine years. He did, however, recover sufficiently in the playoffs to win the Conn Smythe Trophy and the Stanley Cup.

"I don't want to try and philosophize on what happened," said Sather. "We tried to do what was good for Wayne, the Oilers and the NHL. We all would like to be proud of what we do for a living ... I know we'll adjust." In Carson, at age 20, the Oilers are receiving a future superstar. In Gélinas, the Kings' first pick this past June, they have a potentially high scoring left winger. And the three draft picks ensure them of youth in the future. The King abdicated one throne yesterday, then ascended another.

Hockey
in the
Sun Belt

No. 99 will stop at nothing to slow down Toronto's Dave Andreychuk in a playoff game between his L.A. Kings and the Maple Leafs.

Previous page: Gretzky celebrates after breaking Gordie Howe's all-time scoring record with a goal against his former teammates.

While with the Kings, Gretzky teamed up with Hollywood heavyweights John Candy and Bruce McNall to buy Toronto's CFL franchise, the Argonauts.

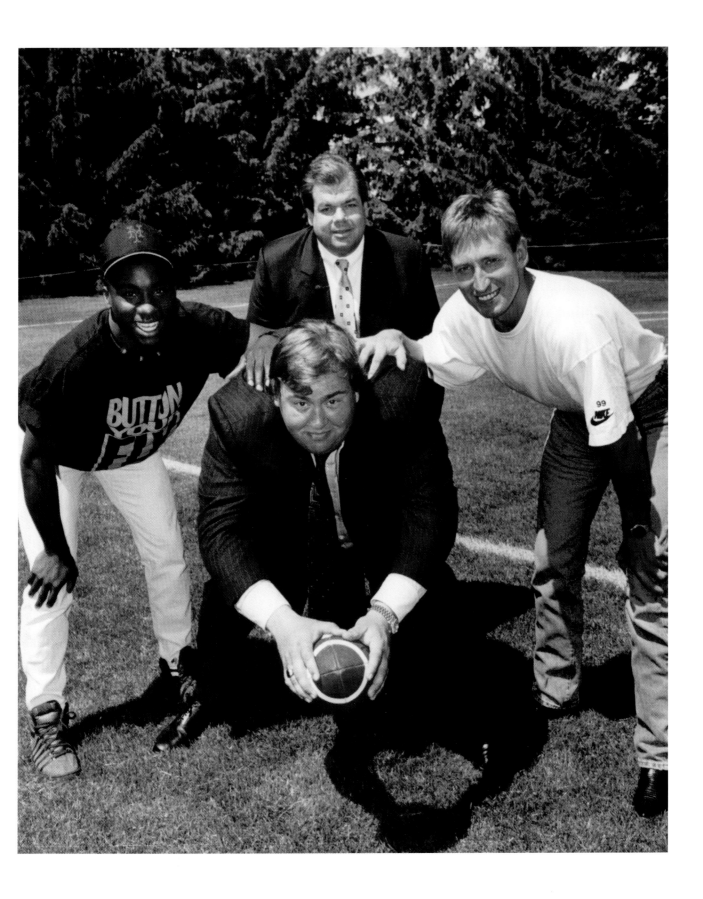

Gretzky scores his 801st goal on Sunday, March 20, 1994, tying Gordie Howe's record, at San Jose Arena against the Sharks. San Jose goalie Arturs Irbe reaches in vain for the puck. Howe took 26 years to do what Gretzky did in just 15 seasons.

Gretzky scores his record-
setting 802nd NHL goal against
the Vancouver Canucks at the
Forum in Los Angeles on
Wednesday, March 23, 1994.
Luc Robitaille (behind Gretzky)
got the assist.

St. Louis

Playing a New Tune

By AL STRACHAN — *Toronto Sun*

"I'm ecstatic," Wayne Gretzky said last night. "I'm thrilled to be going there. It's going to be exciting."

The long-awaited deal was finally made about 5 p.m. MDT, but it didn't get announced until three hours later because it had to be filed to the NHL's head office and given approval. That process was under way late Saturday night when the Kings pulled back and asked for a two-day delay in making the announcement. It was the same deal yesterday — the one announced in the *Sunday Sun*. Gretzky goes to the Blues. Roman Vopat, Patrice Tardif, Craig Johnson and a 1997 first-round draft pick go to the Kings.

By the time the deal was announced, Gretzky had still not talked to St. Louis Blues coach and general manager Mike Keenan, but he had already decided to take part in the Blues' practice here this morning. The Flames play the Blues a week from tomorrow in St. Louis. His linemates? Gretzky didn't know, but when told that Keenan has already suggested it will be Brett Hull and Shayne Corson, he replied: "I sure hope so."

"I'm ecstatic about being able to play for Mike," he said, "and I'm looking forward to playing with Brett."

It may be a reflection of the Blues' frustration in dealing with the Kings that they traded for Gretzky without having had any contract talks. In theory, he could walk away from the Blues this summer when he becomes a free agent without compensation. But Gretzky has never been involved in an acrimonious contract dispute and his advisers are convinced there is so much mutual respect between Keenan and Gretzky they will have no problem arriving at a mutually beneficial arrangement. After all, that's what happened shortly after Gretzky left Edmonton for Los Angeles. The Kings' owner at the time, Bruce McNall, called Gretzky in and worked out a new contract that he said was "the easiest I have ever done."

Gretzky is expected to fill the Kiel Center, which recently has had 4,000–5,000 empty seats most nights. The Blues have the third-

highest ticket prices in the league, not quite $50 on the average. A full building represents an increase of $8 million annually. Every extra playoff night represents a further increase of $1 million. Increased marketing revenues can also be expected. And there's one more advantage: the possibility of a Stanley Cup.

Stanley Cup expectations soared when Gretzky was united with "Iron" Mike Keenan following his February 27, 1996 trade to St. Louis.

Previous page: Gretzky clashes with Leafs captain Doug Gilmour in a 1996 playoff game.

The Great One always loved a visit to Toronto to play the Leafs at Maple Leaf Gardens.

Gretzky scores his first goal with the St. Louis Blues against Vancouver's Kirk McLean.

99 in the Big Apple

Great One even greater

By AL STRACHAN — *Toronto Sun*

NEW YORK — As expected, Wayne Gretzky's opening night in New York was quite a spectacle. But it wasn't the spectacle that the Rangers' fans or even Gretzky himself had been hoping for. For the second time in as many nights, the Rangers fell behind early and then wiped out a two-goal deficit. But this time, they fell behind again and eventually lost 5–2 to the Florida Panthers. "The people have been so good here to me and my family, that I feel so disappointed we didn't win for them," Gretzky said. "I hope it just gets better. Before I came here, people who had never been here asked me about the city and wanted to know if I was crazy. But whether I'm going into a deli or taking my kids to school, the people here couldn't have been nicer." The normally jaundiced New York fans clearly were excited by Gretzky's arrival. During the pre-game warmup, they ringed the glass at the Rangers' end of the rink and snapped pictures of him. Limited-edition programs featuring Gretzky on the cover were all snapped up at $10 each before the game began. Even a taped interview with Gretzky prompted a huge ovation when it was shown on the scoreboard. The fans cheered him lustily during the pre-game introductions and applauded again when he came on the ice for his first shift. But again, as was the case in Boston on Saturday, it was the Rangers themselves who seemed to be the most distracted by all the hoopla. They started extremely slowly, perhaps feeling that with both Gretzky and Mark Messier in the lineup there was no need for a full team effort. But even though both were playing well, neither is good enough to win single-handedly. It turned out that the Rangers didn't even have Messier for the full game. Late in the second period, Florida's Mike Hough had the puck near the boards and, seeing Messier coming, turned his back. When Messier piled into him, Hough went into the boards and Messier got a five-minute checking-from-behind penalty and an automatic game misconduct. Messier's departure left Gretzky in the role of team leader. By that time, he already had racked up his first point as a Ranger. The Panthers took a 2–0 lead in the first

Gretzky arrived in New York determined to win another Stanley Cup.

period, but on a second-period power play Gretzky set up Bruce Driver for a shot that Niklas Sundstrom redirected past John Vanbiesbrouck. In the third period, after killing off Messier's penalty, the Rangers tied the score. But less than a minute later, Brian Skrudland potted his second of the night to put the Panthers back in front and then they added a couple more.

It was a typically strong game by the Panthers and a spotty performance by the Rangers, who have looked brilliant at times and awful at others.

"Are we out of shape?" Campbell asked. "Are we lazy? You've got to ask yourself questions like that after a game like that." Does that include Gretzky?

"I think he played well," Campbell said, "but we have to finish. He finds people. When he was out there, we carried the play, but we didn't score."

As Gretzky said: "It's a matter of getting comfortable with them and them getting comfortable with me. It's a two-way street." Eventually, it should be a street that allows the Rangers to travel a long way.

Regardless of his uniform, Gretzky thrived at Maple Leaf Gardens.

One of many emotional moments in his final season, Gretzky played his last game in fabled Maple Leaf Gardens on December 19, 1998.

Looking cheerful before his last Canadian appearance as an NHL
player, in the nation's capital. The spotlight on Gretzky intensified
as news of his imminent retirement spread.

Following page: Gretzky faces off against Ottawa superstar Alexei
Yashin to begin his final NHL game in Canada.

Captain Canada

August 16, 1996
One final C for Gretzky

By TERRY JONES — *Edmonton Sun*

WHISTLER, B.C. — Glen Sather gave Team Canada a short speech before he added an "Oh, by the way ..." about Captain Canada. "I told them I invited them to a party so they can go to war," he said of his personal philosophy of the golfing, fishing and sightseeing week in Whistler with a few hockey practices thrown in for fun. And, then, as he was winding up, he added the one thing.

"Wayne Gretzky is captain. Anybody have a problem with that?" Nobody stuck their hand up. A few players may have looked out of the side of their eyes at Mark Messier. But by all reports he had a great grin on his face. This may be the last time Gretzky wears a C on his sweater. Messier will keep his C when the two ex-Edmonton Oiler greats play together in New York this year. "Slats just threw it out," Messier said. "Guys kind of looked at each other as if to say, 'No, I don't think anybody is going to have a problem with that.' Wayne has been the Canada Cup captain since 1984," Messier said of the three straight tournaments the team has won. Being the only others who played on all three teams, Messier and Paul Coffey were given an A for their sweaters and Eric Lindros was issued the extra one.

"I don't think it was ever an issue who was going to be captain here," Messier said. And there's no issue about who is going to be captain in New York, either. "In New York, definitely Mark," No. 99 says. "He's the captain of that team."

It ought to be no surprise that the focus found The Great One on the first on-ice day of Canada's training camp. Sather, his sense of stage being perfectly preserved from his days as their coach in Edmonton, put Gretzky and Messier on the same line. The line will remain intact for at least one more day. Why? "They looked like they wanted to play together," he deadpanned. "They were like a couple of teenagers yesterday. They were like a couple of brothers who hadn't seen each other in a long, long time."

Adam Graves was the other guy on the line and the ex-Oiler,

current Ranger, who had never played with Gretzky before, came off the ice with a smile the size of Blackcomb Mountain on his face. "One of these names just doesn't belong," he said of the line. "The thing I have to do is figure out how to cut the puck in two to give each of them half."

Gretzky held court in the narrow dressing room corridor. "We haven't played together in eight years," he said of Messier. "It's a fun time for us." Being back with Sather means something special, too. "I'm excited about it," he said. "It's going to be fun for us with him on the bench. The speech he gave us was one of the same speeches he gave us in the '80s. It's come full circle.

"Maybe in 10 years my kids will play for him. No. Maybe they'll play for Team USA. That was the last question I had before I left," he said of young son Ty. "He wanted to know what team he'd play for."

Gretzky receives the Order of Canada.

Always eager to represent his country, Gretzky produced some memorable moments in the Canada Cup.

In a 1996 World Cup game in Montreal, Team USA's Mike Richter makes a sprawling save to rob the Canadian captain of a goal.

Following page: Hockey's greatest player and its greatest leader (Mark Messier) have a meeting of minds during a practice at the 1996 World Cup of Hockey.

Gretzky arrived at the 1998 Olympic
Games in Nagano, Japan, with high
hopes of attaining one of the few goals
that had eluded him: winning Olympic
Gold.

A disappointed player leaves the ice after Canada loses in a shootout to the Czech Republic in the semi-finals. Gretzky returned home empty-handed after Canada lost the bronze medal to Finland.

The Last Goodbye

An emotional end

By TERRY JONES — *Edmonton Sun*

NEW YORK — There was half a minute left in regulation time when John Muckler called a time out. At the time Gretzky was fighting with everything he had to control his emotions. "That was the most emotional time. That's when it really hit me that I was done. I looked up and said, 'My goodness, I've got 30 seconds to go.' That's when it hit me." Muckler, when he called the time out, called Gretzky over. "John called a time out there and kind of waved me over. He's got a daughter who is about to give birth in Edmonton and he called a time out with 30 seconds to go and I came over and he said, 'I got to tell you something.' I said, 'What?' He said, 'I just had a grandson today. And you've got to get the winner for him.'" Gretzky looked around the interview room. "I didn't get it for him today. And I know it's the right time."

During those final moments of the game Mark Messier and Paul Coffey stood beside the boards in the Zamboni entrance. They, like those who have covered his career and watched Gretzky write storybook ending after storybook ending, were saying the stage is set for the guy again. He's gonna get the winner. "It seemed like everything in his career seemed to be like that," said Messier. "He almost scored a goal toward the end of the game and Paul and I were sitting by the boards. We said, 'How many times did we see this happen?' He came off the bench, the puck was on his stick and he scored the goal. And it almost happened again." Except storybook as this afternoon was, it didn't have the storybook ending: Jaromir Jagr scored at 1:22 of overtime. The Pittsburgh Penguins beat the New York Rangers 2–1. In his last at-bat, the mighty Gretzky had struck out. Well, not really. He played great. Gretzky played like he did in the all-star game. Problem was, the guys he was playing with in this game weren't all-stars. They were Rangers.

"I wish I could have been Michael Jordan, hitting that last shot to win the championship. But that wasn't going to happen," said Gretzky. In the seventh minute of the first period Gretzky set up

Niklas Sundstrom but the left-winger fanned. On the first shift of the second period he set up Sundstrom spectacularly and again he failed to finish. Twice on a mid-period shift he made magic on plays involving John MacLean, including creating a two-on-one, and both times MacLean messed them up. Finally, with 29.9 seconds left in the period, Gretzky threw a classic breakout pass that his two defensemen converted into a goal. Assist No. 1,963. Point number 2,857. Gretzky kept creating and getting chances, including a glorious opportunity he created for himself late in the game.

"It was a tough game for me today," said Gretzky. "I tried to do my best. I went home last night at 8. I said, 'I'm leaving.' My dad said, 'Where are you going?' I said, 'It used to be, in the old days, you told me to get to bed. Now you're asking why I'm leaving.' I wanted to approach the game the best I could, but it was hard. What made it even harder was my teammates were trying so hard. I think Niklas is such a great young player and a great young gentleman, I felt sorry for him at times. I knew he was nervous. When you are nervous like that, it means a lot of things. It means you are a good person. I think it was a tough game for my teammates but they enjoyed it."

Gretzky said he knew he wasn't going to get hit by anybody on the Penguins. But just in case he got hauled down on a breakaway, he had a little chat with referee Bill McCreary on his way to the ice for the third period. "I said, 'OK, one thing.' He says, 'What?' I said, 'Even if we're close, no penalty shot.' I said, 'Even if the guy tackles me, I don't want a penalty shot.'"

Two of the best players the game has ever seen, Mario Lemieux (above) and Mark Messier (right), show their respect for the Great One at his final game.

Proud grandfather Walter and young Trevor Gretzky.

The Gretzky family at the final game.

Following page: An emotion-filled Gretzky waves goodbye and reacts to a video presentation following his last game in the NHL.

Wayne leads his teammates around the ice during ceremonies following his last game in the NHL.

The Gretzky File

Career Stats

Final Statistics

Season, Team	GP	G	A	Pts
1979-80, Edm-ac	79	51	86	137
1980-81, Edm-ab	80	55	109	164
1981-82, Edm-abd	80	92	120	212
1982-83, Edm-abd	80	71	125	196
1983-84, Edm-abd	74	87	118	205
1984-85, Edm-abd	80	73	135	208
1985-86, Edm-ab	80	52	163	215
1986-87, Edm-abd	79	62	121	183
1987-88, Edm	64	40	109	149
1988-89, LA-a	78	54	114	168
1989-90, LA-b	73	40	102	142
1990-91, LA-bc	78	41	122	163
1991-92, LA-c	74	31	90	121
1992-93, LA	45	16	49	65
1993-94, LA-bc	81	38	92	130
1994-95, LA	48	11	37	48
1995-96, LA-StL	80	23	79	102
1996-97, NYR	82	25	72	97
1997-98, NYR	82	23	67	90
1998-99, NYR	70	9	53	62
Totals	1487	894	1963	2857

a-won Hart Trophy as NHL's Most Valuable Player.
b-won Art Ross Trophy as NHL's highest scorer.
c-won Lady Byng as most gentlemanly player.
d-won Lester Pearson award as NHL's outstanding player.

Playoff Statistics

Season, Team	GP	G	A	Pts
1979-80, Edm	3	2	1	3
1980-81, Edm	9	7	14	21
1981-82, Edm	5	5	7	12
1982-83, Edm	16	12	26	38
1983-84, Edm-y	19	13	22	35
1984-85, Edm-yz	18	17	30	47
1985-86, Edm	10	8	11	19
1986-87, Edm-y	21	5	29	34
1987-88, Edm-yz	19	12	31	43
1988-89, LA	11	5	17	22
1989-90, LA	7	3	7	10
1990-91, LA	12	4	11	15

1991-92, LA	6	2	5	7
1992-93, LA	24	15	25	40
1995-96, StL	13	2	14	16
1996-97, NYR	15	10	10	20
Totals	208	122	260	382

y-won Stanley Cup
z-won Conn Smythe Trophy as Most Valuable Player of the Stanley Cup
playoffs.

All-Star Statistics

YEAR	G	A	Pts
1980	0	0	0
1981	0	1	1
1982	1	0	1
1983-x	4	0	4
1984	1	0	1
1985	1	0	1
1986	1	0	1
1988	1	0	1
1989-x	1	2	3
1990	0	0	0
1991	1	0	1
1992	1	2	3
1993	0	0	0
1994	0	2	2
1996	0	0	0
1997	0	1	1
1998	0	2	2
Totals	12	10	22

x-Chosen MVP.
There was no game in 1987 because Rendez-Vous 87, a two-game series between Team NHL and the Soviet Union, replaced the All-Star game. There was no game in 1995 due to the owners' lockout.

Trophy Case

Stanley Cups: 1984, 1985, 1987, 1988
Hart Memorial Trophy (regular season MVP): 1980, 1981, 1982, 1983, 1984, 1985, 1986, 1987, 1989
Art Ross Trophy (regular season scoring champion): 1981, 1982, 1983, 1984, 1985, 1986, 1987, 1990, 1991, 1994
Conn Smythe Trophy (Stanley Cup playoffs MVP): 1985, 1988
Lester B. Pearson Award (NHL's outstanding player, selected by players): 1982, 1983, 1984, 1985, 1987
Lady Byng Memorial Trophy (most gentlemanly player): 1980, 1991, 1992, 1994
Emery Edge Award (best plus-minus rating): 1983, 1984, 1985, 1987
All-Star MVP: 1983, 1988, 1999
Chrysler-Dodge/NHL Performer of the Year: 1985, 1986, 1987
Lester Patrick Trophy (outstanding service to hockey in the United States): 1994
Canada Cups: 1984, 1987, 1991

Career Highlights

Ontario Hockey League

1976-77: Peterborough Petes, three assists in three games

1977-78: Sault Ste. Marie Greyhounds, 70 goals and 112 assists in 64 regular-season games and 6 goals and 20 assists in 13 playoff games. Started season with No. 19, switched to No. 14 and then to No. 99 at the suggestion of general manager Murray "Muzz" MacPherson. OHA Rookie of the Year and second-team all-star.

World Hockey Association

1978: Signed a multiyear contract with the Indianapolis Racers as an underage junior, June 12, 1978.

Had 3 goals and 3 assists in 8 games for the Racers before being traded to the Edmonton Oilers with Peter Driscoll and Ed Mio for cash and future considerations in November 1978. Had 43 goals and 61 assists in 72 regular-season games for Oilers and 10 goals and 10 assists in 13 playoff games. WHA Rookie of the Year and second-team all-star.

National Hockey League

1979: Reclaimed by Edmonton as an underage junior prior to 1979 expansion draft.

1979-80: Was ruled ineligible in 1980 for the Calder Trophy, which goes to top NHL rookie, but won the Hart Trophy as NHL's MVP. Second team all-star. Became youngest player in NHL history to score 50 goals in a season. Scored first NHL goal in his third game (10-14-79) vs. Vancouver (Glen Hanlon).

1980-81: Led league in scoring to win first Art Ross Trophy. Named to first all-star team. Won second Hart Trophy.

1981-82: Set NHL record for goals (92), assists (120) and points (212) in regular season. First player to score 200 points in a season. Won his third Hart Trophy , second Art Ross Trophy and named to first all-star team.

1982-83: Set record for assists (126) and broke record for playoff assists (26) and points (38). Won his fourth Hart Trophy and third Art Ross. First team all-star.

1983-84: Set NHL record for longest consecutive points streak from start of season (51 games: 61 goals, 92 assists). Set record for most goals in a season, including playoffs (100), and most shorthanded goals in a season (12). Captained Oilers to first Stanley Cup. Won Hart and Art Ross trophies. First team all-star.

1984-85: Set NHL assist record (135). Set NHL playoff record for assists (37) and points (47) and won Conn Smythe Trophy. Set NHL record for points in a season, including playoffs (255). Registered 1000th career point. Won Stanley Cup, Hart Trophy and Art Ross Trophy. First team all-star.

1985-86: Set NHL records for assists (163) and points (215). Set NHL record for assists in a season, including playoffs (174). Won Art Ross, Hart Trophy. First team all-star.

1986-87: Scored 500th goal (November 22, 1986, vs. Vancouver). Won Stanley Cup, Hart Trophy, Art Ross Trophy. First team all-star.

1987-88: Became NHL's all-time assist leader (1,050). Won second Conn Smythe Trophy. Won Hart and Art Ross trophies. Second team all-star.

1988-89: August 9, 1988: Traded to Los Angeles with Mike Krushelnyski and Marty McSorley for Jimmy Carson, Martin Gelinas, L.A. Kings' first-round draft choices in 1989 (acquired by New Jersey, who selected Jason Miller), 1991 (Martin Rucinsky) and 1993 (Nick Stajduhar) and cash. Tied NHL record for most 50-goal seasons (9). Scored his 600th career goal (November 23, 1988, vs. Detroit). Won ninth Art Ross Trophy. Second team all-star.

1989-90: Became NHL's all-time leading scorer (1,851 points), passing Gordie Howe on October 15, 1989. Won eighth Art Ross Trophy. Second team all-star.

1990-91: Broke own NHL record with 23-game assist streak. Scored 2,000th career point (October 26, 1990). Scored 700th goal (January 3, 1991, vs. New York Islanders). Won ninth Art Ross Trophy and second Lady Byng Trophy. First team all -star.

1991-92: Passed Marcel Dionne for second place on all-time NHL goal scoring list with goal 732 (December 21, 1991). Recorded career assist 1,500 (March 4, 1992). Won third Lady Byng Trophy.

1992-93: Missed first 39 games with back injury. Played 1,000th career game. Had 16-game goalless drought, longest of his career. Recorded point 2,300 (March 6, 1993) vs. Edmonton. Led NHL in playoff scoring (40 points). First player to score 100 career playoff goals.

1993-94: Became all-time leading goal scorer (802) by passing Gordie Howe (March 23, 1994, vs. Vancouver). Won tenth Art Ross Trophy, fourth Lady Byng Trophy. Second team all-star.

1994-95: Recorded career point 2,500 (April 17, 1995, vs. Calgary).

1995-96: February 27, 1996: Traded to St. Louis for Craig Johnson, Patrif Tradif, Roman Vopat, St. Louis's fifth-round draft pick (Peter Hogan) in 1996 amateur entry draft and first-round pick (Matt Zultek) in 1997 draft.

1996-97: July 21, 1996: Signed as a free agent by New York Rangers

1998: January 18, 1998: Became the leading scorer in NHL All-Star Game history with two assists at the 1998 North America vs. World game in Vancouver. February 1998: Played for Team Canada in the Winter Olympics in Nagano, Japan

1999: March 1999: Gets 1,072nd goal, leading goal-scorer in hockey April 1999: Retires from NHL

NHL Records

Wayne Gretzky holds or shares 61 records listed in the League's Official Guide and Record Book: 40 for the regular season, 15 for the Stanley Cup playoffs and six for the All-Star Game.

Regular Season Records (40)

Goals (6)

Most goals: 894 (1,485 games)
Second: 801 - Gordie Howe, 26 seasons, 1,767 games

Most goals, including playoffs: 1,016 - 894 regular season and 122 playoff
Second: 869 - Gordie Howe, 801 regular season and 68 playoff

Most goals, one season: 92 - 1981-82, 80-game schedule
Second: 87 - Wayne Gretzky, 1983-84, 80-game schedule

Most goals, one season, including playoffs: 100 -- 1983-84, 87 goals in 74 regular season games and 13 goals in 19 playoff games.
Second (tied): three players

Most goals, 50 games from start of season: 61 -- 1981-82 (Oct. 7, 1981 to Jan. 22, 1982, 80-game schedule); 1983-84 (Oct. 5, 1983 to Jan. 25, 1984, 80-game schedule)
Next (third): 54 -- Mario Lemieux, 1988-89 (Oct. 7, 1988 to Jan. 31, 1989, 80-game schedule)

Most goals, one period: 4 - (tied with 10 other players) Feb. 18, 1981, at Edmonton, third period (Edmonton 9, St. Louis 2)

Assists (6)

Most assists: 1,962 (1,485 games)
Second: 1,102 - Paul Coffey, 19 seasons, 1,320 games
Most assists, including playoffs: 2,222 - 1,962 regular season and 260 playoff
Second: 1,226 - Paul Coffey, 1, 090 regular season and 136 playoff

Most assists, one season: 163 - 1985-86, 80-game schedule
Gretzky holds top seven positions, tied with Mario Lemieux for eighth

Most assists, one season, including playoffs: 174 - 1985-86, 163 assists in 80 regular season games and 11 assists in 10 playoff games
Gretzky holds top ten positions, tied with Mario Lemieux for eleventh

Most assists, one game: 7 - (tied with Billy Taylor) done three times - Feb. 15, 1980 at Edmonton (Edmonton 8,

Washington 2); Dec. 11, 1985 at Chicago (Edmonton 12, Chicago 9); Feb. 14, 1986 at Edmonton (Edmonton 8, Quebec 2)
Second: 6 - 23 players

Most assists, one road game: 7 (tied with Billy Taylor) - Dec. 11, 1985 at Chicago (Edmonton 12, Chicago 9)
Second: 6 - four players

Points (4)
Most points: 2,856 - 1,485 games (894 goals, 1,962 assists)
Second: 1,850 Gordie Howe, 1,767 games (801 goals, 1,049 assists)

Most points, including playoffs: 3,238 - 2,856 regular season and 382 playoff
Second: 2,010 - Gordie Howe, 1,850 regular season and 160 playoff

Most points, one season: 215 - 1985-86, 80-game schedule
Next (fifth): 199 - Mario Lemieux, 1988-89, 80-game schedule

Most points, one season, including playoffs: 255 - 1984-85; 208 points in 80 regular season games and 47 points in 18 playoff games
Next (sixth): 218 - Mario Lemieux, 1988-89; 199 points in 76 regular season games and 19 points in 11 playoff games

Overtime Scoring (1)
Most overtime assists, career: 15
Second: 13 - Doug Gilmour, 16 seasons

Scoring by a Center (6)
Most goals by a center, career: 894, 20 seasons
Second: 731 - Marcel Dionne, 18 seasons

Most goals by a center, one season: 92 - 1981-82, 80-game schedule
Second: 87 - Wayne Gretzky, 1983-84, 80-game schedule
Third: 85 - Mario Lemieux, 1988-89, 80-game schedule

Most assists by a center, career: 1,962, 20 seasons
Second: 1,040 - Marcel Dionne, 18 seasons

Most assists by a center, one season: 163 - 1985-86, 80-game schedule
Gretzky holds top five positions
Most points by a center, career: 2,856, 20 seasons
Second: 1,771 - Marcel Dionne, 18 seasons

Most points by a center, one season: 215 - 1985-86, 80-game schedule
Gretzky holds top four positions

Scoring by a Rookie (1)
Most assists by a player in one game in his first NHL season: 7 - Feb. 15, 1980, at Edmonton (Edmonton 8, Washington 2)
Second: 6 - Gary Suter, April 4, 1986 at Calgary (Calgary 9, Edmonton 3)

Per-Game Scoring Averages (4)
Highest goals-per-game average, one season: 1.18 - 1983-84, 87 goals in 74 games

Second (tied): 1.15 - Mario Lemieux (1992-93, 69 goals in 60 games) and Wayne Gretzky (1981-82, 92 goals in 80 games)

Highest assists-per-game average, career (300 min.): 1.321 - 1,962 assists in 1,485 games
Second: 1.183 - Mario Lemieux, 881 assists in 745 games

Highest assists-per-game average, one season: 2.04 - 1985-86, 163 assists in 80 games
Next (eighth): 1.52 - Mario Lemieux, 1992-93, 91 assists in 60 games

Highest points-per-game average, one season (among players with 50-or-more points): 2.77 - 1983-84, 205 points in 74 games
Second: Wayne Gretzky

Scoring Plateaus (12)
Most 40-or-more-goal seasons: 12 in 20 seasons
Second: 10 - Marcel Dionne in 18 seasons

Most consecutive 40-or-more-goal seasons: 12 - 1979-80 to 1990-91
Second: 9 - Mike Bossy, 1977-78 to 1985-86

Most 50-or-more-goal seasons: 9 (tied with Mike Bossy) - Gretzky in 20 seasons and Mike Bossy in 10 seasons
Third: 6 - Guy Lafleur in 17 seasons

Most 60-or-more-goal seasons: 5 (tied with Mike Bossy) - Gretzky in 20 seasons and Mike Bossy in 10 seasons
Third: 4 - Phil Esposito in 18 seasons

Most consecutive 60-or-more-goal seasons: 4 - 1981-82 to 1984-85
Second: 3 - Mike Bossy, 1980-81 to 1982-83

Most 100-or-more-point seasons: 15 in 20 seasons
Second: 10 - Mario Lemieux in 12 seasons

Most consecutive 100-or-more-point seasons: 13 - 1979-80 to 1991-92
Second: 6 - six players

Most three-or-more-goal games, career: 50 - 37 three-goal games; 9 four-goal games; 4 five-goal games
Second: 39 - Mike Bossy in 10 seasons (30 three-goal games, 9 four-goal games)
Most three-goal games, one season: 10 (done twice) - 1981-82 (six three-goal games; three four-goal games; one five-goal game) and 1983-84 (six three-goal games, four four-goal games)
Next (third): 9 - Mike Bossy (1980-81, six three-goal games, three four-goal games) and Mario Lemieux (seven three-goal games, one four-goal game, one five-goal game)

Longest consecutive assist-scoring streak: 23 games - 1990-91, 48 assists
Second: 18 - Adam Oates, 1992-93, 28 assists

Longest consecutive point-scoring streak: 51 games - 1983-84 (Oct. 5, 1983 to Jan. 28, 1984, 61 goals, 92 assists for 153 points)
Second: 46 - Mario Lemieux, 1989-90 (39 goals, 64 assists)

Longest consecutive point-scoring streak from start of season: 51 - 1983-84; 61 goals, 92 assists for 153 points (Oct. 5, 1983 to Jan. 28, 1984)

Playoff Records (15)

Individual Playoff Records (7)
Most playoff goals, career: 122
Second: 109 - Mark Messier

Most assists in playoffs, career: 260
Second: 186 - Mark Messier

Most assists, one playoff year: 31 -1988 (19 games)
Gretzky holds top three positions

Most assists in one series (other than final): 14 - (tied with Rick Middleton) 1985 conference finals (six games vs. Chicago)
Second: 13 - Doug Gilmour, 1994 Conference Semifinals (seven games Toronto vs. San Jose) and Wayne Gretzky, 1987 Division Semifinal (five games vs. Los Angeles)

Most assists in final series: 10 - 1988 (four games, plus suspended game vs. Boston)
Second: 9 - three players

Most assists, one playoff game: 6 - (tied with Mikko Leinonen) April 9, 1987 at Edmonton (Edmonton 13, Los Angeles 3)
Next: 5 - 11 players

Most assists, one playoff period: 3 - Three assists by one player in one period of a playoff game has been recorded on 70 occasions. Gretzky has had three assists in one period five times. (Ray Bourque, three times; Toe Blake, Jean Beliveau, Doug Harvey and Bobby Orr, twice.)

Playoff Points (4)
Most points, career: 382 - 122 goals and 260 assists
Second: 295 - Mark Messier, 109 goals and 186 assists

Most points, one playoff year: 47 - 1985 (17 goals and 30 assists in 18 games)
Second: 44 - Mario Lemieux, 1991 (16 goals, 28 assists in 23 games)

Most points in final series: 13 - 1988 three goals and 10 assists (four games plus suspended game vs. Boston, three goals)
Second: 12 - four players

Most points, one playoff period: 4 - (tied with nine other players) April 12, 1987 at Los Angeles, third period, one goal, three assists (Edmonton 6, Los Angeles 3)

Playoff Shorthanded Goals (2)
Most shorthanded goals, one playoff year: 3 - (tied with five other players) 1983 (two vs. Winnipeg in Division Semi-Finals, won by Edmonton, 3-0; one vs. Calgary in Division Finals, won by Edmonton 4-1)

Most shorthanded goals, one playoff game: 2 - (tied with eight other players) April 6, 1983 at Edmonton (Edmonton 6, Winnipeg 3)

Playoff Game-Winning Goals (1)
Most game-winning goals in playoffs, career: 24
Second: 19 - Claude Lemieux

Playoff Three-Or-More-Goal Games (1)

Most three-or-more-goal games: 10 (8 three-goal games, 2 four-goal games)
Second (tied): 7 - Maurice Richard (4 three-goal games, 2 four-goal games, 1 five-goal game) and Jari Kurri (6 three-goal games, 1 four-goal game)

NHL All-Star-Game Records (6)

NHL All-Star-Game Goals (3)

Most all-star-game goals: 13 (in 18 games played)
Second: 11 - Mario Lemieux (in 8 games played)

Most all-star-game goals, one game: 4 - (tied with three players) 1983 Campbell Conference

Most all-star-game goals, one period: 4 - 1983 Campbell Conference, third period

NHL All-Star-Game Assists (1)

Most all-star-game assists, career: 12 - (tied with four players)

NHL All-Star-Game Points (2)

Most all-star-game points, career: 25 - (13 goals, 12 assists in 18 games)
Second: 22 - Mario Lemieux (11 goals, 9 assists in 8 games played)

Most all-star-game points, one period: 4 - (tied with Mike Gartner and Adam Oates) 1983 Campbell Conference, third period (four goals)